When Donkeys Fly

Written by:
Ginger Hodge

Illustrated by:
C.B. Markham

Designed by:
Kim Hall

Hi, Rochel!
I've heard great
things about you and
hope to meet you soon ☺
Hope you will always follow
your dreams and
be brave enough to
Fly Donkey Fly!

This book is dedicated to the people who support us,
and the kid in all of us who is brave enough
to follow a dream.

This book belongs to:

Rachel

First Edition
Copyright © 2008 by Ginger Hodge
All Rights Reserved.

Written by: Ginger Hodge
Illustrations by: C.B. Markham
Design by: Kim Hall

ISBN 13: 978-0-9815967-0-9
ISBN 10: 0-9815967-0-3
Library of Congress Control Number: 2008902207

Inspiring the world
one page at a time.

DONKEYFLY
PRESS

1st Printing June 2008
Published by Donkeyfly Press
East Coast Creative Group, USA
Printed in USA

www.whendonkeysflybook.com

When Donkeys Fly

What does it all mean?

When I was a child, if someone wanted to do something
that seemed impossible, he or she was told,
"that will happen when donkeys fly".
Since most people believe donkeys never fly,
they would also believe these things would never happen.

I often wondered what would happen if one,
just one donkey, found a way to take flight.
Imagine all of the wonderful things that would
suddenly become possible
When Donkeys Fly.

I went to my first game
and wanted to try...

1

...to hit the ball
and make it fly.

"But you're a girl,"
one boy did cry.

"You can play baseball
when donkeys fly."

One day a horse
went galloping by.

Now that is something
I'd like to buy.

But my father
couldn't understand why.

"You'll have a horse
when donkeys fly."

I saw a plane
flying way up high.

Then a parachute
floated in the sky.

When I told my mother
I wanted to try,

she said I could...

...when donkeys fly.

I turned on the TV
and what did I spy?

A contest with models
strolling by.

12

I wish I could do that
I said with a sigh.

"You'll be Miss America
when donkeys fly."

A beautiful boat
came sailing by.

I'll have one of those
before I die.

But they are very, very
expensive to buy.

"You'll own a boat
when donkeys fly."

We went to Washington
to see this guy.

WASHINGTON OR BUST!

His job seemed important,
one I wanted to try.

"President? Never,
you're way too shy."

"You'll work in the White House
when donkeys fly."

Then I looked up,
and what did I spy?

Not a bird, not a plane, but
with the blink of an eye.

20

Now I can do whatever I try...

TO TRY:
astronaut
president
deepsea explorer
princess
teacher
archeologist
mom
scientist
doctor
astronomist
artist
actress
author
lawyer
movie producer
ballet dancer
professor
dog trainer

...because I have seen
a Donkey Fly.

What you don't know
is this story is true.

It's not just about me.
It is about you.

You can do anything
you want to do...

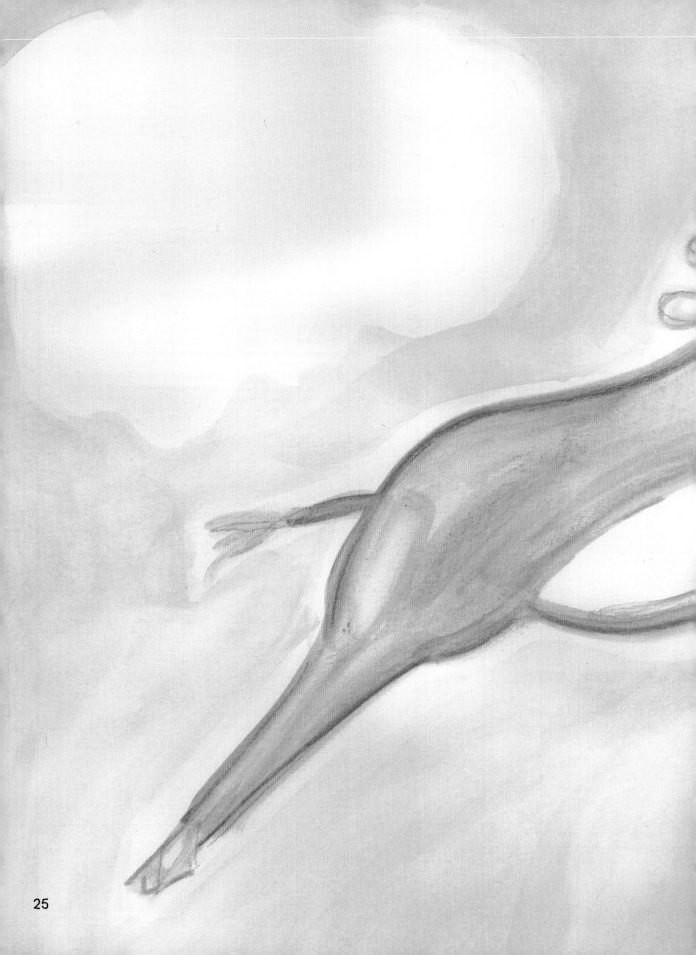

...because now you've seen a Donkey Fly too.

Note from the Author:

I hope that you enjoyed the book and were
happy to see the Donkey Fly in the end.
But did you know that he was there the whole
time? He was waiting and watching to make
sure that everything was always possible.
Go ahead. Take a peek. See if you can find
The Flying Donkey hiding on every page spread.

Need a hint?
Visit our website at
www.whendonkeysflybook.com

Who is the dog
on the front of the book?

The dog on the front cover is a Labrador Retriever
mix named Sadie Hawkins Hodge.
She was rescued from an animal shelter when she
was 18 months old. When Ginger adopted her,
Sadie could already sit, whisper, stay and shake.
Her hobbies include fetching, licking, eating treats
and riding on the boat. Sadie's best friend is Diana,
Ginger's niece. Her favorite toy is a squeaky giraffe
and her favorite food is sliced bread. She has even
been known to borrow loaves of bread on occasion
from the kitchens of unsuspecting neighbors.
Everybody loves Sadie.
She is a good dog.